LETTER TO NANDINI

Part 1

Gloria Sarker

Dedication to my Ancestors and Spirit Guides

This is a poetry book with lots of expression. The best way to communicate exactly what is our mind. There is nothing better to sit down with a pen and paper and write our expression. We can write anything that comes to our mind, listen our heart and name the feeling with honestly and sincerely. Finally enjoy the journey.

Letter to Nandini- Part 1
All rights reserved
© Gloria Sarker, Melbourne 2023
ISBN: 978-0-6454016-3-9

Poem 1

I call you Nandini
Would you like to google it?
Can you reach the hole?
Under the gold
Mining of Coles?

Nandini you live in my core
Light in the dark
Robi Tagore called you "Rokto Korobi".
I call you Nandini.

Red roses are your necklace.
Yellow roses are your earrings.
Red wine in the sunshine
Glimpse in your smile.
Beauty is her name.
I call you Nandini.

Nandini I only want you.
It's not my need.

My morality is higher than my desire.
My love is my decision.
Nandini you are my joy.
Shine like bright light.

Poem 2

Nandini you can stay a little longer.
My heart is pounding.
I am wondering.
A lot in my mind
Time does not flow.
I have no clue.
Love never stays.
I can't walk away.
Can you please stay?

I put myself down.
I count.
Many times, I am down.
I ignore me.
I forgive me.
I am silly and crazy.
I don't know how to
find peace and harmony.
My sadness does not go away.
My pen goes on many pages.
Deeper and deeper
My heart and soul
Don't talk.
All are in my head.
I love my sadness.

Poem 3

Nandini you gave me a space
A time
A place
I can hide.
I hide somewhere.
No one can find me.

I can hide my hurt.
My pain
My Suffering
I celebrate my misery.
my separation.

Nandini, I walk on the beach.
The ocean takes away my footsteps.
I can hide.
Your ignorance
All is sour and bitter.
I sit on the sand.
On the dark
Sun does not see my tears.

Nandini, please come close to me.
I can't sink in the sand.
Water does not take me away.
Your silence
Days and years
You don't care.
I hide my tears.
Love never comes near.

Poem 4

Smile Nandini please smile.
Your smile
shows your happiness.
your joy and care.

Nandini is happy.
be peaceful.
you are beautiful.
like the bush flowers
The amazing colors.
My all best wishes to you
All love for you
You are in my thoughts.
All day long.

Your silence makes me slow down.
To be silent my headspace
To see myself
My mind
My heart
My sadness
My trauma.
My overthinking is a pain.
I welcome the rain.
Let's it make flood and cyclone.
and all fountains
Let all my pain and sorrows.
flash away.

Let the green grows in my soil.
My heart space.

The mountains flow with flowers
Let my words breeze!
Let the love enters my life.

Nandini, please
Be smile always.
I hide my cry
My hurt
on your smile.

Poem 5

Nandini you are the one.
in my heart
The spring is in here.
The unseen will be seen.
They all are awake.
They are talking to me.
They are in my words.
The color
New leaves
New life
Come, everyone!
Welcome.
Dance with me
in the spring.

Let the summer dry all!
The sand
The desert
makes me cry.
Tears flow from the eyes
I open my heart.
My words come.
I write
with an unsettled mind.

Poem 6

Nandini, how I make you more beautiful?
Seeing you in the spring
I find you.
Deep breath
My repetitive old patterns
I go after it again.
No change inside me
I only see the beauty.
You are beautiful.
Let my words come.
My pen and papers
My poems and songs
All for you.

The color of the Spring,
all precious stones and crystals
All jewellery
All happiness to you.
My heart is for you.
My love is for you.
Please come close.
Come to home.
I love what I know.
I fear to choose the unknown.

Poem 7

Nandini, where have you been?
It's been a long wait.
All the seasons
All the years
Waiting and waiting long many years.

I know you are coming.
I know your steps.
You are on your way.
All mornings
All afternoon
All my sleepless nights
My summers
My winters
My springs
I give you all.
You come to me.
I am being impatient.
My songs
My poems
All my writing is over.
My love
You are not here.
I give away my joy and happiness.
I live in misery and sadness.
My love
Come and live with me!
You bring joy and happiness.
My love
Come
Stay with me.

Poem 8

Nandini you were walking towards me.
In the desert
Red sands
Black color
Blue tops
I notice.
You were carrying a bottle of water.
In your hand.
You were walking towards me.
Curly hair
Black dark eye
You were barefooted.
Walking on the sands

I was looking at you.
I was thinking.
and watching the old ancient love
Your love takes my heart away.
You come close to me.
You smile.
you passed by
You are walking towards your path.
I thought.
You were walking towards me.
I notice it was not me.

Poem 9

Nandini, what if I don't meet you?
I would have not known love.
Your present taught me how to love.
Perhaps how to love myself.
I do exit.
I do have a voice.
My present matters
I have the desire.
To walk with you in the moonlight
Singing songs.

Nandini you awaken me
My Trauma
My trigger
My sadness
and darkness
You came to me in the rain.
You walk in the rain.

My mornings
My sleepless nights
Life takes away us.
You said to love yourself first.
We must
Meet on the way half!
You told me to find my happiness.
You teach me.
How to love myself?

I went into the deep of my trauma.
and I find a way out.

to embrace the process
and I find the beautiful gift underneath my darkness.
Nandini, you showed me how to love.
I live my life.

Poem 10

I want you Nandini.
I see love in your eyes.
I want you slowly.
There is no rush.
I am not running to you.
I want to walk there.
I want to enjoy the journey.
The path
The process
The beauty of waiting
The benefit of fear and doubt.

Nandini the time has come.
The green sign
The words
The birds
The Moon
All emotions
Long time to get there.
to see you again.

I love to see you again.
Where we meet first?
I have time to wait.
I make time to look at you.
Your eyes, smiles, and vibes.
I left behind all my success,
fame, and possessions.
You are the only one.
in front of me.
I love to walk with you.
I wait for you.

Poem 11

Nandini today I love myself.
I value myself.
Today I chose myself.
Today I do what I like to do.

Today you wanted to tell me.
You want me because I am worthy to have.
I have control over my life.
I am not chasing you.

Nandini, I express my love to you.
I listen to my heart.
I watch my behavior
I watch your actions.
I have in between my strength and vulnerability.
I am being humble.
I maintain my boundaries.

Don't overvalue!
or undervalue.
Nandini's time to self-talk
and talk with you.
I meet you halfway.
I listen to you.
We both have an equal
balance of giving and receiving.

Poem 12

Nandini you can trust me.
My all heart and all love is for you
I am healed.
I am grown.
I am mature.
I come a long way.
I am complete.
I am independent.
I am fulfilled by myself.

Nandini my heart is ready.
Wide open
I control my life.
I am connected.
I live a life.
that I was wanted.
I treat myself like the queen.

I keep my word.
I am ready to love.
No drama
No baggage
No envy
No jealousy.

I am organized.
I am a good planner.
I know my plan.
I am a master manifester.
I am intentional.
I am determined.

I wait for what I want.
I act and get what I want.
Love comes easily and effortlessly.
Nandini we are in the same boat.
We are on the same journey.

Poem 13

Nandini, I know you are delay.
You are taking your time to come home.
You are doing what needs to be done.
You are clearing your mess.
Your long-lasting family
Children
Possessions
Friends
Work
and I am on a new adventure.

In a new life
New place
New work
All are new to me.
I am waiting for you.
I am impatient.
and restless
I want your connection.
I want to hear your voice.
Your words
You touch.

Nandini, why are you silent?
I know you tell me everything.
You are preparing your way.
to join me
I want to hear from you.
I want you.
You are taking a long way to come.

Poem 14

Nandini, I want to make you happy.
I want to see your smile.
When you say " I want to cry"
I will bring you the ocean.
The water from all the fountains and falls
Every raindrop from the sky.
All colors from the rainbow.

When you say "Leave me alone
I want to be myself."
I stay away.
I wait.
I wait longer than I can.
I walk in the mountains.
The green grass
The sweet waters
All the morning dews
I bring you all the glitter and gold.
When you say, "I want to laugh."
Your smile fades away from the sun.
The moon shines from a far.

When you say "I am sad"
I sit with you.
I bring all the dreams from my ancestors.
all the old souls
I dance with you.

The ocean waves break the beach.
All the cycles bring the winds.
With flash lightning

When you are angry.

I bring you all the red roses.
When you say
"Let me love you"!
I come along with a gentle heart.
kind words
I hold you with warmth.

Poem 15

Nandini, I surrender.
I express my feelings to you.
I want to know you more.
I want to love you.
I am vulnerable.
I am weak.
I am in love with you.

Nandini, I want to know you more.
My heart is dancing.
I remember you.
You are in my thoughts.

Nandini, I surrender.
I want you more.

Poem 16

Nandini my head has no space.
Headspace has no harmony.
My heart is disturbed.
My throat is choked.
Time for auto-writing.
Let my words come in a blue color
With my vision and truth
My imagination.

Let me talk to you!
I am thinking about you.
I know your journey.
Your memories
Your belongings
Your passion and possessions
Your duties and tasks.

Nandini you are living the life
That past is holding you tight.
You can't live in the present.
Where is the future?

Let the past be behind us!
Rest and peace
Bring happy memories!
Grace and gratitude.

Nandini, I don't know where I stand.
Why are you calling me?
Why are you ghosting me?

Poem 17

Nandini how long do I have to wait?
When the time comes?
When I am ready?
When you are ready?

Nandini has been waiting for that day.
when you finally come into my life.
I ask for that day.
The wait is longer than expected.

The longer it gets.
The desire becomes stronger.
When I see you next
I know you will come one day.
One day you hold me tight.
Holding hand
Soft gentle touch
Kiss
Talk all night.

Nandini you are not ready.
I am not ready.
We are working our present days.
Our past divided us.

Our expression becomes hot and cold.
Anger and sadness
Patient and impatient
Laugh and tear.
We live in the present and past.
That's why
love has not arrived.

Poem 18

Nandini, when you will arrive?
When you are ready to come into my life?
What offers do you have?
What do you want?
What are doing now?
Why are you thinking a lot?
Why have you disappeared?
Why do you want to come back?

Nandini's time has not been ready.
Perhaps we live in a different world.
Perhaps we have another mission.
Desire and passion
that needs separation.

Poem 19

Nandini beholds my beloved.
You have given the authority.
To step on the serpents
and the evil scorpions.
You can command them free from evil.
So, do I
I command my heart full of love.

You are powerful.
Nothing can hurt you.
Your flesh is weak.
You are a divine protection.
Flash and blood
Cast the demons.
You have all the weapons.

Nandini hears your voice.
Listen to your heart!
Follow your spirit!
Speak in a new tongue.

Nandini's enemies will rise against you.
To be defeated before you.
They will come in one way.
and cast in seven ways.
Let your truth be spoken!
Transformed yourself.
Renew your mind each day!
Let not your heart be troubled!
Be strong.
Be bold.
Nandini stays on the path of righteousness.

Poem 20

Nandini healing is a process.
It's a journey.
Enjoy the journey!
Embrace this with bad and good!
Embrace your pain.
The wound left scars
Deep bruise
Accept it with no shame or anger.
Be optimistic.
Focus on your purpose.
This a transition
Like a butterfly ready to fly.

Nandini you want to heal
But you love your pain.
Your emotions and addictions
All about relationships.

Your poor choice
The repeat cycles.
Your reaction and rejection
Self-talk and false belief.

You have shown your strength.
Thanks, pain.
Thanks, shame.
I am nacked.
I am selling my success.
In the market.

Poem 21

Nandini, I have a choice.
I am faithful.
I chose the success.
I release my old beliefs.
My old self-negative talks
doubt and fear.

Nandini I can see without judgment.
I am connected to my infinite.
I am connected to my happiness.
Safety and satisfaction are with me.
Abundance follows me.

I am unique.
I am loved.
I am worthy.
I am humbled.
I am open to learning.

Nandini, I walk into a new door.
I love to have a surprise.
I am connected to myself.
I am fulfilled.
I am enough.
I am complete.
I am grateful.
I am love.

Poem 22

Nandini, I am standing in front of a waterfall.
I am in my reality.
With my body, mind, and soul.
They are together and balanced.

I am within me.
It's my time to shine.
It's my time to talk.
I am connected to my purpose.
I follow my heart.
I keep work on me.
I am safe.
I am brave.

Poem 23

Nandini are you waiting for an apology?
Who was unfair to you?
Who was cruel and brutal?

Nandini honor yourself.
Walk away from betrayal.
Fall in love with yourself!
Invest for your happiness.

Nandini, you know your worth
You stand on your ground.
You have a sound.
You express.
You shout.
You have a voice.
You have a choice.

Poem 24

Nandini Fire Fire, and Fire
The fire burning into my heart.
My whole heart is burning.
No more cry
No more upset
I am over it.
I am over everything.

I go back to my past.
My repetitive pattern
My cigarettes and alcohol
My laziness
My sadness
No motivation
procrastination
over and over
I keep trying.
I am being sober.

Poem 25

Nandini breaks up is not break up.
It's a transition.
The transition between two journeys
two cycles.

Let one exit and rest!
Recover the shadow!
Underneath the shadow
There is a gift.
Rest and receive.

Let us not hate and anger.
Takes your place in your heart.
Pain and suffering in your body.
Let life digest easily.
Let love dwell in your heart.

Nandini breaks up is not a break.
It's a matrix.
Between two dimensions
Two realities
No judgement
Only witness
Let your spirit guide you.
Let your mind free.
More empty
Stay still.
Let your ego free.
as it knows it's time is short.

Nandini let peace and kindness.

live forever.
Let forgiveness enter!
Let love allows you.
to cross the bridge
between the two journeys.

Nandini, it is not a breakup.
It was never.
It will never
Let your spirit evolve!
and live forever.

Poem 26

Nandini let go of the past
Don't hold the anger.
It increases the scar.
Pain and suffering.
It does not serve you.
Your present and future.

Nandini let the past rest.
Learn the liaison.
You are worthy.
Let the spirit help you.
Let your heart fill with joy.
Love and light
Shine your day.
Let grace and growth enter your life.

Nandini you conquer your fear
Guilt and shame
No more worries
or overthink.

Nandini let go of the past
The present is precious.
Count your breath!
Receive the bless.

Poem 27

Nandini, I have done my part.
My task and duties
I work hard.
I find the gift under my shadow.
when I am in sorrow.

Nandini the reality was different.
I was broken.
Down and fearful
I was unloved and unworthy.

Nandini I am working on me.
I have hope.
One day someone will walk by my side.
One day we grow together.
One day we explore the world.
One day we understand each other better.

Nandini, I am worthy to have.
I am filling my cups.
I am fulfilled by myself.
I am growing each day.
I am satisfied without you.
I bring my joy.
I love myself.
Nandini you are worthy to have.
We love and live forever.

Poem 28

Nandini, I tell you.
Have a dream.
Be Grounding
Be Balancing
Be Mirroring
Fearing
Gut feeling
Polarizing
Cause and effect
Wish fulfillment.
Truth Revealed
The third eye opened
Heart allows.
Close eyes
Vision follows.
Take actions!
Drive emotion
Light to light
Spirit guide
Good night
Sleep right
Deep breath
Bear feet
Relax and wait.
Joy and peace
Be brave and bold.
Enjoy this life.
and be evolved.

Poem 29

Hello Nandini
Do you know Nandini?
Why there is the hole in Solomon's soul?
Why did Jacob send Uriah to be killed?
Ahad needed rehab with Zazabel
Mary Magdalene poured oil on Yousuah's sole.
Why did Judah kill Jesus?

Nandini Amazon burning.
Rohingya running.
Mining progressing
Rothschild smiling.

Nandini you hoping.
I am praying.
We are crying.
Yeshua coming
Peace restoring
Evil in Abyss
Love is flowing.

Nandini, you're free to return home.
when you need comfort
Nandini up your head
Look at the world!
Straight into your eye
Never wake your love
Until it arrives.

Poem 30

I name you Nandini
I call you again and again.
Nandini you are beautiful.
You are shining in the bright light.
You are my sunshine.

I saw you in the shopping center
You were present there.
By yourself.

I was watching you.
I approach you
I spoke to you.

Nandini you walk away from your destination
I was in myself.
sitting on my jigsaw puzzles
Learning my secret
Finding my talents
Knowing the meaning of life
I find my purpose.
I give away my talents.
Joy comes from giving.
I gave you all.

Nandini you are a new being now
Transforming, challenging
Visioning, performing, and working.

Nandini you came across a long way
Will go further ahead.
Take a rest.
Do your best.

Poem 31

Nandini, I am thinking of you.
All the time
You have no time.
No contact
No text
It is my time to talk to you.

Love flows in one direction.
You make me real.
Slow down
Slower
Delay to respond.
No fear
All are dry and desert.
I cry for cigarettes and brandy.
Give me a call.
No more ignorance
Nandini you mean a lot
Please give me a call.

Poem 32

Nandini, do you know?
How would I feel?
When I see you next?

Nandini my heart wants to see you.
I am confused.
I am nervous.
My eyes look for you.
In the crowd
Can I see you? Where are you?
Why can't I see you?

Nandini, I live in a dream.
It's my illusion.
I want to see you more.

Poem 33

Nandini, I know you Nandini.
You are my dream girl.
You are the one.
I want to see you once more.

I want to touch you.
Smell you.
Feel your softness.
You are adorable.
All my unconditional love is only for you.
I want to walk with you.
Under the moonlight
On the beach
Spring
Fallen stars.
Cool breeze.
The angels smile.
Air whispers
Our loves shine forever.

Poem 34

Nandini, I proclaim my love.
I am your secret admirer.
I am passionate about you.
I want to share my life with you.
All my love for you
I receive the same from you.
We share life, joy, and adventure.
We thrive.

Poem 35

Nandini Nandini
You are not invisible anymore.
I can see you now.
I can touch you.
I can tell you.

Nandini you are fearless.
You are brave.
No one can read you.
You are fierce.
You are jealous.

Nandini you are free to go.
If you don't want to know
No romance
I wait.
You can return.
You can wait.

Poem 36

Nandini you want me
You called me.
You are not close.
You are not far.
I don't know.
What do you want?
I don't know what meant to be.
I walk in the flow.

I want to see you.
Let our past in the past
Let us release our burden!
We are free.

Nandini are you ready?
Take your time.
Slow down and shine.
In your good days
Remember the past.
Sad and sorrows.

Poem 37

Let me touch you Nandini.
Let us be free from everything!
That holding us back.
Let us stand on the mountain!
Touch the blue skies.

Let's not worry!
Let's not be anxious about the past and future!
All our dreams must come true.
Our wishes are on the way.
We never walk in the past
We never repeat the walk.
We engage.
We are looking forward to the change.
We surrender.
We awake.
Our spirit guides us.
Reward and peace with us
Let's not be afraid!
Be bold.
Be brave.

www.ingramcontent.com/pod-product-compliance
Lightning Source LLC
Chambersburg PA
CBRC090836010526
44107CB00050B/1634